How To Convince Your Parents You Can...

Care For A Pet Ferret

Tamra Orr

P.O. Box 196
Hockessin, Delaware 19707
Visit us on the web: www.mitchelllane.com
Comments? email us: mitchelllane@mitchelllane.com

Printing   1   2   3   4   5   6   7   8   9

A Robbie Reader/How to Convince Your Parents You Can...

Care for a Pet Bunny	Care for a Pet Mouse
Care for a Pet Chameleon	Care for a Pet Snake
Care for a Pet Chimpanzee	Care for a Pet Tarantula
Care for a Pet Ferret	Care for a Potbellied Pig
Care for a Pet Horse	Care for a Wild Chincoteague Pony

Library of Congress Cataloging-in-Publication Data
Orr, Tamra.
  Care for a pet ferret / by Tamra Orr.
      p. cm. — (A Robbie Reader—How to convince your parents you can...)
  Includes bibliographical references and index.
  ISBN 978-1-58415-660-4 (library bound)
  1. Ferret—Juvenile literature. I. Title.
  QL737.C25O77 2008
  636.976'628—dc22
                                                                    2008002240

ABOUT THE AUTHOR: Tamra Orr is a full-time writer and author living in the Pacific Northwest. She has written more than 50 books for children and families, including *Orlando Bloom*, *Ice Cube*, and *Jamie Foxx* for Mitchell Lane Publishers. She is a regular writer for more than 50 national magazines and a dozen standardized testing companies. Orr is mother to four and life partner to Joseph.

PHOTO CREDITS: Cover—The Animal Welfare League of Alexandria; pp. 1, 3—JupiterImages; pp. 4, 7, 15, 18, 23, 24, 27—Kyla Hills/Hugawoozel; pp. 14, 21, 22, 26—Riley Hills/Hugawoozel; p. 8—Arizona Game and Fish Department via Cronkite News Service; p. 10—William Munoz/Photo Researchers; p. 12—David R. Frazier/ Photo Researchers; p. 28—Inkrat773/Creative Commons; pp. 29–32—Jeff Vanuga/ Corbis.

TABLE OF CONTENTS

Words in **bold** type can be found in the glossary.

Owning a ferret can be a lot of fun, but ferrets require a lot of training. To get your ferret to walk on a leash, you'll first need to train it to wear a harness (ferrets can slip right out of a collar). Then you can introduce it to the great outdoors. Have plenty of treats handy, and reward your ferret for being so brave.

FERRETS ARE FUN!

You've seen one. You want one. Now all you have to do is get your parents to agree.

There is no doubt about it. Ferrets are very cute animals. They love to play. They are fun to watch. They are the best hide-and-seek players ever! They love being held and touched.

It is easy to understand why you would want a ferret for a pet. Before you decide if you should have one, you need to learn about this funny animal. It is the only way to know whether a ferret is the right pet for you and you are the right owner for a ferret.

Ferrets love to play even more than they love to sleep, and they sleep a lot—as many as 18 hours a day. When they are awake, they are ready for action! If they are kept in their cages all day and their basic needs are not met, they will get sad and sometimes even sick. They have to be out of their cages at least four hours a day. Six hours is even better. If you are going to be in school all day, playing with your friends all afternoon, doing homework all evening, and then heading off to bed, a ferret is the wrong pet for you. It has to have a lot of time out of its cage, so it can play, play, play!

A ferret wants to run and explore. It is a curious animal. It is also quite smart. It always wants to know what is around the next corner. What is in the cupboard? What is behind the door? What is under the couch? What is on the other side of that little hole in the wall? It wants to find out.

A ferret also wants to play with toys. It wants to grab that sock you left on the floor and attack it. Most of all, it wants to spend time with you. This means you have to take a lot of responsibility caring for your pet. You have to make time to come home and play with it—every single day. You can't leave it alone over the weekend. This is a pet that really needs your time and attention. Are you willing to do that? Are your parents willing to help you? If you do not have their support, owning a ferret may be more work than you can handle.

Ferrets are also friendly. They want to play with you—and with any other pets you might have. Some pets will like a ferret. Others will not! Most of the time, ferrets get along with dogs and cats, but

not always. It depends on what your dog or cat is like. Some may want to play. Others will get angry or jealous. They might hurt your ferret.

Some pets do not do well with ferrets at all. Birds, hamsters, guinea pigs, and rabbits are good examples. Your ferret may just want to play, but it could end up hurting one of these pets. Ferrets are meat eaters. They may think one of your smaller pets is a quick meal.

*fun*FACTS

The word *ferret* comes from a Latin word for "little thief." That is the perfect name for an animal who loves to steal things when you aren't looking.

Like any pet, ferrets are cute—but they can also be very demanding! Make sure you know what you are getting into before you talk to your parents. Finding things out after you get a pet is not the way to go!

Duncan is an albino ferret. He has white fur and red eyes.

The black-footed ferret is the only ferret native to North America. It is extremely rare. The ferrets sold as pets are a distant cousin of the black-footed ferret. Pet ferrets were bred from European weasels that were tamed hundreds of years ago.

Chapter Two

FACTS ABOUT FERRETS

What type of animal is **related** (ree-LAY-tud) to a ferret? If you think it is a rodent like a mouse, rat, or hamster, you are wrong. Ferrets are actually related to weasels and minks.

It is easy to see why some believe a ferret is a rodent. It looks like one. It is long and skinny. Males are usually 15 to 16 inches long. They weigh between two and five pounds. Females are a little bit smaller. They are 13 to 14 inches long. They weigh between a half pound and two and a half pounds. Letting your parents know how small and light ferrets are might help them agree to let you have one.

Some think that ferrets are wild animals. They believe ferrets belong in the wild and not in homes as pets. That is not true either. Ferrets are **domesticated** (doh-MES-tih-kay-ted), which means they are raised to be pets. They need to be taken

Ferret kits at about two weeks old. Mother ferrets give birth about 42 days after mating. Usually, litter size is from six to nine kits. The babies will begin to grow fur when they are nine days old. Their eyes will open after three to five weeks.

care of to live. In the wild, they would not be able to survive.

There is a myth that says ferrets do not have a backbone or spine. If you watch one run around and play, you might see how the myth started. Ferrets can move, stretch, and turn in amazing ways. The myth is untrue—ferrets do have spines. They also have muscles that help them bend and twist in a lot

of directions. They are also able to squeeze through very small holes.

One ferret myth is true. They do have an unusual scent. It is often described as musky. Like skunks, they put out a smell if they feel frightened or threatened. Most ferrets are **descented** (dee-SEN-ted) before they are sold, but even then, sometimes a slight odor remains. Some people do not mind the smell. They know that most pets, including cats and dogs, have a unique odor.

Others think the way to get rid of the smell is to give their ferret a bath every few days. This doesn't work. Too many baths will make a ferret's skin dry, and the ferret will make more oil—the source of the smell—to help **moisten** (MOYS-in) its skin. Keeping the litter box clean will help keep the smell down. Making sure your ferret gets the right food and takes vitamins will also make a difference.

When choosing a ferret, look for one that is used to being held. Also, be sure it is legal in your town to keep a ferret as a pet.

FINDING A FERRET

If you decide that you want a ferret, be sure it is legal in your town to keep one as a pet. Some places do not allow ferrets at all, and other places require you to fill out special paperwork. If it is legal and your parents are willing to think about it, how do you find a ferret? You have a couple of choices.

Was your first idea a pet store? That is where most people think to go to buy a ferret. This is not always the best idea, though. Some of the ferrets found in pet stores were taken from their mothers when they were too little. This is hard on them. They also have not been around people enough to be comfortable with them. This means they may be scared of humans. If they are too frightened, they might bite or hurt anyone who tries to touch them.

Instead of a pet store, have your parents help you look in your city's newspaper and phone book to see if there are any ferret **breeders** (BREE-derz) in the area. These are people who specialize in raising **generations** (jeh-nuh-RAY-shunz) of animals safely and carefully. They know a great deal about making sure animals are not taken away from their families until they are ready. They also spend time handling and talking to the animals so that each one is used to being around humans.

Look in the ads in your local newspaper. Maybe someone is selling or giving away their ferret because they can no longer keep it.

Another place to look for a ferret is at your local animal shelter. Often the ferrets found there have already spent time around people. They are older, so you do not have to worry about training them to use a litter box or not to bite. They will be happy to have a good home.

What should you look for in a ferret? You want to make sure it is healthy. It should have:

- An alert and curious personality
- Clear eyes
- A shiny, thick coat
- Strong teeth

Find out the ferret's age. As a general rule, these animals live five to ten years. You will want to get a pet that still has years left to enjoy.

You also need to think about equipment for your ferret. Your parents will want to know what a ferret needs. If you have a list ready, your chances of getting a "yes" might go up.

fun **FACTS**

Ferrets love sandboxes! They bury their toys and then kick the sand around until they find them again.

Spike stretches after a long nap. The floor of his cage is covered with a soft rug.

Your ferret's cage should have lots of ramps on which your ferret can play, plus cozy beds and hammocks in which it can get its daily eighteen hours of sleep. The cage should also have heavy bowls for water and food, and a litter box.

Ferrets are known to take your things. Some of a ferret's favorite things to steal are socks, keys, bottle caps, hair brushes, and pencils. They will hide them in the smallest of places.

Muccles enjoys the soft tunnels and warm bed in his cage.

YOU'LL NEED THESE THINGS FOR YOUR NEW FERRET

- Wire mesh cage: For one ferret, you need a cage at least 2 feet high by 2 feet wide by 2 feet long. Be sure to put something on the floor of the cage to protect its feet. You can use wood chips, or a blanket or rug.

- Heavy food and water bowls: Ferrets delight in dumping their bowls, so get heavy ones that are hard to flip over.

- Basket, box, or plenty of soft, clean rags: Put these at the bottom of the cage for the ferret to snuggle and sleep in. Rags must be washed weekly.

- Litter box and litter: The litter box must be washed weekly and the litter changed daily.

- Ramps and tubes: You do not have to have these in your cage, but they do make it more fun for your ferret.

- Treats: Your ferret will love eating treats, and you will need them for any training you give your ferret.

- Food and vitamins (VY-ta-minz)

All the ferret basics can be found in pet stores. You can also look at garage sales and online for used equipment. If you get your ferret from a breeder, you can ask about places to find supplies. You can check with your shelter for help too.

Ferrets require more care than a lot of other pets. One of the most common ferret diseases affects the **adrenal** (uh-DREE-nul) **glands**, and surgery is often required to correct the condition. Ferrets can also catch the flu, just like people, and will sneeze and wheeze if they have it. Pay close attention to your ferret when it is healthy, and you'll quickly be able to spot any signs of trouble if it gets sick.

FEEDING AND CARING FOR FERRETS

Caring for a ferret is hard work. It is important to know that right from the beginning.

Taking care of any pet takes time and effort. When it comes to ferrets, however, it takes even more work than usual. That is something you really need to think about before you choose to get a ferret. Are you willing to take the time to give it the care it needs? Are your parents willing to help? You will need their help. There are many things you will need to do for your ferret. You must:

- Clip its nails once a week (this will take an adult's help, so talk to your parents about this).

- Clean out the litter box once a day and refill it with clean litter.

- Clean your ferret's ears once a month (this also will take an adult's help).

- Give your ferret a bath once every two to three months (this may take help from your entire family—some ferrets love baths but some do not).

- Take it to the vet at least twice a year to have its teeth cleaned and to get a checkup.

- Give it vitamins on a regular basis.

- Train it to use a litter box (and remember that it is not an **instinct** for a ferret to use a litter box, the way it is for a cat, so your ferret may still have accidents).

- Train it not to bite. Most of the time when ferrets nip, they do it in play. They have thick skin, so they don't know biting hurts. You will though! To teach your ferret not to bite, experts suggest responding by spraying water or blowing in the ferret's face, covering its face, or immediately putting it back into its cage.

- Keep it from digging. Ferrets love to dig. Houseplants are a favorite. Litter boxes can be fun too. The same method you use to show your ferret not to bite should be used whenever it digs into something it shouldn't.

Most of the time when ferrets do something wrong, like biting or digging, it is because they are bored. They want something fun to do. That is why

Muccles doesn't mind taking a bath, but some ferrets hate it. You can buy ferret shampoo, or you can use shampoo made for babies or kittens.

you need to get down on the floor and play with your ferret every day!

Ferrets need to eat often, and they need to eat protein. You should make sure that your ferret always has dry food available. There are foods made just for ferrets. Your **veterinarian** (veh-truh-NAYR-ee-un) can tell you the names of some good ones. Do not give your ferret cat or dog food just because you have some at home. It is not good for them and can make them sick. Also remember that your ferret is a lot like a kid—it will eat as many treats as you give it, so limit them. Use them just for training in the beginning, and then hand them out only now and then. Your ferret also needs clean water to drink. You should change the water and wash out the water bowl at least once a day. Twice is better.

Ferrets must see the veterinarian on a regular basis. There are diseases that can kill them. You have to make sure they stay as healthy as possible.

Muccles, Spike, and Duncan get a treat for good behavior. Ferrets learn better when they are rewarded for doing something right, rather than being punished for doing something wrong.

Spike and Duncan sneak a taste of their vitamins. Liquid vitamins can be added to dry food to help keep your ferret healthy and its coat shiny.

One of the biggest health problems for ferrets is a result of eating the wrong thing, like a tiny toy part, a bit of Styrofoam, or a packing peanut. This can cause a **blockage** (BLAH-kidj) in their **intestines** (in-TES-tinz). If this happens, they will get sick quickly. The best way to prevent blockages is to make sure there is nothing on the floor where your ferret plays. You need to keep an eye on your ferret when it is out of its cage.

Like other ferrets, Muccles enjoys dressing up. Ferrets like feeling cozy—and wearing ferret clothes can make them feel safe and secure. It can also give their owners a good chuckle.

IS YOUR FAMILY A FERRET FAMILY?

As you can see, having a ferret can take a lot of work and time. That is why you have to learn as much about the pet as you can before you make a decision. You need to see what your parents think of the idea too.

Ferret-proofing any room your pet will be in is very important. You must make sure all holes and doorways are blocked. Windows must be closed and locked. Cupboard doors have to be locked because ferrets are smart enough to open them. The floors must be free of anything the ferrets might eat. If you have furniture in the room, check it carefully because ferrets love to crawl up inside and can get hurt if you sit down. Your parents may have some great ideas for ferret-proofing a room. They had to do almost the same thing when you and any of your brothers or sisters were babies. The job is even

harder with a ferret, because ferrets are so good at getting into small spaces.

Ferrets are cute, cuddly creatures. Just one look at the "flat ferret" pose is enough to make anyone want one. In this position, the ferret gets as low to the ground as possible. It looks like a speed bump on the floor. It crawls on its belly to you, looking for attention. If you do

Duncan, in a flat ferret pose, begs for attention.

Muccles gets snuggles from Riley (left) and Kyla (below).

Whenever you take your ferret outside, it is important to put on its harness and leash. This will keep your little explorer out of trouble.

not reach out and pet it, it will often tap you on the foot with a paw as if to say, "Hi! I'm here. I'm cute. Play with me!"

Another ferret move is sure to make you laugh. First it will begin to hop around like it has springs in its feet. Next it will arch its back like a cat and then open its mouth wide. Finally it will begin to swing its head back and forth and then chirp or hiss. You may think your ferret is sick . . . but it isn't. It is doing the ferret dance of joy!

The ferret dance of joy is also called the weasel war dance. When a ferret gets excited, it will bounce all around, open its mouth, and puff out its tail. Sometimes it will flip completely over in midair.

Yes, it means your ferret is happy.

Why not get down and join it in the dance? You could even try doing it first for your parents. Maybe it will be enough to get them to say, "Sure! Let's become a ferret family!"

Books

Bach, Richard. *Curious Lives: Adventures from the Ferret Chronicles*. Charlottsville, Virginia: Hampton Roads Publishing Company, 2005.

Doudna, Kelly, and C. A. Nobens. *Frisky Ferrets*. Edina, Minnesota: ABDO Publishing Company, 2007.

Gelman, Amy, and Andy King. *My Pet Ferrets (All About Pets)*. Minneapolis, Minnesota: Lerner Publications, 2000.

Horton-Bussey, Claire. *101 Facts About Ferrets*. Milwaukee, Wisconsin: Gareth Stevens Publishing, 2002.

McNicholas, June. *Ferrets (Keeping Unusual Pets)*. Port Melbourne, Victoria, Australia: Heinemann Library, 2003.

Works Consulted

Bossart, Dick. *The Ferret Owner's Manual.* www.thechipster.com/fert-man.html

Horton-Bussey, Claire. *101 Facts about Ferrets*. Milwaukee, Wisconsin: Gareth Stevens Publishing, 2002.

McLeod, Lianne. *Ferret Facts.* http://exoticpets.about.com/cs/ferrets/a/ferrets101.htm?p=1

McLeod, Lianne. *Ferret-Proofing Your Home.* http://exoticpets.about.com/od/ferretcare/a/ferretproofing.htm?p=1

So You Wanna Get a Ferret?
http://www.soyouwanna.com/site/syws/ferret/
ferretfull.html

Web Addresses
Animal Welfare League of Alexandria
http://www.alexandriaanimals.org/~awla/adoption_
stories2.cfm?story_id=6
Critter Library: Common Ferret Diseases
http://www.animalnetwork.com/Critters/library/
diseases/dis_heart.asp
Defenders of Wildlife: Black-footed Ferret
http://www.defenders.org/wildlife_and_habitat/
wildlife/black-footed_ferret.php
The Fast Track for All Your Ferret Needs
http://www.ferretdepot.com/ferrets.shtml
Ferret Care, Information, Chat, Ferret Supplies,
and More
http://www.everythingferret.com/index.htm
Ferret Central
http://www.ferretcentral.org/
Hugawoozel
http://www.hugawoozel.com/
Humane Society of the United States: Ferret
http://www.hsus.org/animals_in_research/species_
used_in_research/ferret.html
News & Information for Ferret Lovers
http://www.weaselwords.com/

adrenal (uh-DREE-nul) **glands**—Organs that produce chemicals that keep the body healthy.

blockage (BLAH-kidj)—The state of being blocked or having something in the way.

breeders (BREE-derz)—People who raise animals for sale or show.

descented (dee-SEN-ted)—Having odor-causing glands removed.

domesticated (doh-MES-tih-kay-ted)—Adapted to living with people.

generations (jeh-nuh-RAY-shunz)—Groups of living beings born around the same time. Parents are in one generation; their children are in the next generation.

instinct (IN-stinkt)—A natural desire.

intestines (in-TES-tinz)—A long tube between the stomach and the anus.

moisten (MOYS-in)—To make wet.

musky (MUS-kee)—Having the heavy odor of musk.

myth (MITH)—An invented story or idea.

neuter (NOO-ter)—To remove a male's reproductive organs.

related (ree-LAY-tud)—Connected.

rodent (ROH-dent)—A small mammal with sharp front teeth for gnawing.

spay (SPAY)—To remove a female's reproductive organs.

veterinarian (veh-truh-NAYR-ee-un)—An animal doctor.